Merry Christmas 1991
Tom, Helen & Eddie

CELEBRATION II: CLEVELAND IN COLOR

CELEBRATION II:
CLEVELAND IN COLOR

By JENNIE JONES

Copyright ©1991 by Jennie Jones, Inc.

All rights reserved. This book or any part thereof may not be reproduced in any form whatsoever, whether by graphic, visual, electronic, filming, microfilming, tape recording, digital scanning or any other means except in the case of brief passages and no more than two visual graphics embodied in critical reviews and articles, without the prior permission of the publisher. Write to:

JENNIE JONES, INC.
One Cleveland Center, Cleveland, Ohio 44114-1724

ISBN 0-9617637-2-8

PREFACE

IN RESPONSE to many requests, this second photographic essay, *Celebration II: CLEVELAND IN COLOR*, follows *CLEVELAND: A CELEBRATION IN COLOR*, first published in 1986. The hopes of the past, present and future are seen in the man-made structures that house Cleveland's activities. *CLEVELAND IN COLOR* represents a personal sojourn through the dramatic physical changes witnessed over the last five years.

I would like the reader to note that the interiors of our great public and commercial buildings often equal the beauty of their facades. The men and women who went before us took great pleasure in superior craftsmanship, architectural detail and rich building materials

As an architectural photographer, I have been privileged to work on two of Cleveland's major building sites–Tower City Center and Society Center. The transformation of Terminal Tower into the Tower City Center and The Avenue represents recognition of the value of our past as we prepare for the future. The construction of Society Center, now the tallest building between New York City and Chicago, represents our belief in the future of Cleveland.

Even though I find great pleasure in seeing architectural structures and details through the lens of a camera, I believe it is the men and women who designed and built these structures that leave their true mark on this or any city. The men and women who actually built these dreams are seldom known by name to the general public, but their effort, and sometimes their lives, leave a lasting memorial and testament to the courage and excellence of human effort. To climb into the sky with them is both humbling and exhilarating.

And so this book is dedicated to those leaders who have striven to take this great city into the future and to those craftsmen, both past and present, who have clothed these dreams in stone and steel, concrete, glass and marble. It is the people of Cleveland who are to be celebrated.

The effort and dedication required to record the changing face of Cleveland would not have been possible without incredible support. My deepest thanks go to my husband, Trevor and my children, Rob and Bronwyn, for their constant enthusiasm and patient understanding. Special recognition must be given to Jim Janos, Mark Destino, Rick Sherlock, Crain Smith and Julie Pettibone who worked grueling hours with me on many of the sites, as well as Ellen Palmer who untiringly manages the business side of my work. John Szilagyi, who designed the format and layout of both books, is always encouraging and exciting to work with. There are so many others who have made this work possible–thank you all.

I especially thank Cleveland for presenting me with a canvas so enticing!

– *JENNIE JONES*

INTRODUCTION

AS INTERNATIONAL rivalry for economic development becomes more intense, cities around the world are searching for new, special or unique incentives to give them advantages in the global competition which they face.

Quality of life has become one of the most important ingredients in attracting residents and industry alike. Private businesses considering relocation find their executives and employees not only seek good neighborhoods and affordable housing but much more. Diversified entertainment and cultural institutions as well as world-class sports and recreational facilities are now essential in attracting new residents.

The greater Cleveland area is fortunate to have laid a foundation to match these demands for the future. Throughout the area's history of nearly 200 years, committed public officials, business and community leaders, developers, city planners, architects, volunteers and visionaries have established a tradition of excellence that is second to none.

Few cities can match our showcase of cultural and arts institutions. The Cleveland Arts Consortium embraces 21 major museums, visual arts and performing arts organizations.

University Circle is the home of many of our greatest cultural assets including the world renowned Cleveland Museum of Art, the Natural History Museum, the Western Reserve Historical Society and the Garden Center. In addition, Cleveland Play House, the oldest professional resident theater in the nation, now operates three stages in its spacious facility very near University Circle.

The Cleveland Orchestra is the most frequently recorded orchestra in the United States. For three decades it has been one of our finest exports, reaching audiences in Europe and the Far East through tours, recordings and broadcasts. Over 70 years of distinguished history includes open air concerts at the Blossom Music Center during the summer and performances at Severance Hall in University Circle during the winter months.

Downtown at Playhouse Square, the Ohio, State and Palace theaters have been elegantly restored to their former splendor. This 7000-seat complex is home to Cleveland's professional opera and ballet companies, as well as the Great Lakes Theater Festival. In addition, the Playhouse complex annually offers entertainment by major companies out of New York City including plays, musicals and special presentations.

To enrich our cultural choices further, Clevelanders and visitors alike enjoy outstanding rock and roll entertainers, as well as contemporary music performers, at the Front Row Theater, the Coliseum, Public Hall and the Cleveland Stadium. The soon-to-be-open Rock and Roll Hall of Fame and Museum will teach and entertain in excess of 500,000 visitors each day.

For year-round sports enthusiasts, Cleveland is the proud home of four major sports teams – the Browns, the Cavaliers, the Indians and the Crunch, all of which provide major league entertainment and excitement.

Located on Lake Erie, Cleveland enjoys an abundance of fresh water for swimming, boating and fishing. Four distinct seasons provide a wealth of outdoor activities including tennis, swimming, hiking and biking, as well as skiing, tobogganing and ice skating. Quick access is available to the 19,000-acre MetroPark system, known as the Emerald Necklace, which surrounds the greater metropolitan area. The Cuyahoga Valley National Recreation Area and the 800-acre Holden Arboretum offer educational and hiking opportunities which are unequalled in any area.

The quality of life is further enhanced by the availability of diverse and affordable housing, all easily accessible from the downtown area. Unlike residents of many metropolitan communities, most Greater Clevelanders reside within a 20-40 minute drive to work or to most of the diverse activities which are available. There is excellent public transportation and convenient access to the highway network.

Cleveland offers internationally renowned health facilities with the Cleveland Clinic, University Hospitals, Mt. Sinai Medical Center and Cleveland Metropolitan General Hospital. All together, there are 31 outstanding hospital and health facilities available in the Greater Cleveland Area.

Greater Cleveland ranks among the finest cities for higher education. Nineteen institutions are located within 30 miles of the downtown area. Case Western Reserve University, located in the cultural hub of University Circle, has had eight Nobel prize winners among its outstanding faculty and students. It is the largest private research university in Ohio, generating over $100,000,000 a year in research projects. Other outstanding educational institutions include John Carroll University in University Heights and Cleveland State University, which is located in the heart of Cleveland's business community. CSU has recently expanded its campus to include a Music and Communications Building as well as a modern Convocation Center with a 12,000-seat arena.

Celebration II: CLEVELAND IN COLOR, Jennie Jones' second pictorial essay on Cleveland, describes the diversity and beauty of this community as seen by a nationally known photographer. She moved here in 1978 and has spent the last 13 years capturing Cleveland through her lens. The Greater Cleveland Growth Association is proud to offer this beautiful collection to residents and visitors alike as an invitation to share our pride in a city that is ready for the challenges of the future.

RICHARD W. POGUE, Chairman
Greater Cleveland Growth Association

PHOTOGRAPHIC INFORMATION

The photographs were taken with the following camera systems:
35mm – Olympus OM4T
120 – Mamiya RZ67
4x5 – Sinar F1 / Schneider lenses
Fujirama 6x7 Panoramic Camera

The film used was:
35mm – Fuji 100 Daylight
120 – Fuji 100 Daylight / Tungsten
4x5 – Polaroid Prochrome / Daylight
      Polaroid Prochrome / Tungsten

The book was printed by:
The Emerson Press, Cleveland, Ohio
Color separations were also by The Emerson Press
Book design by: John Szilagyi, Inc.

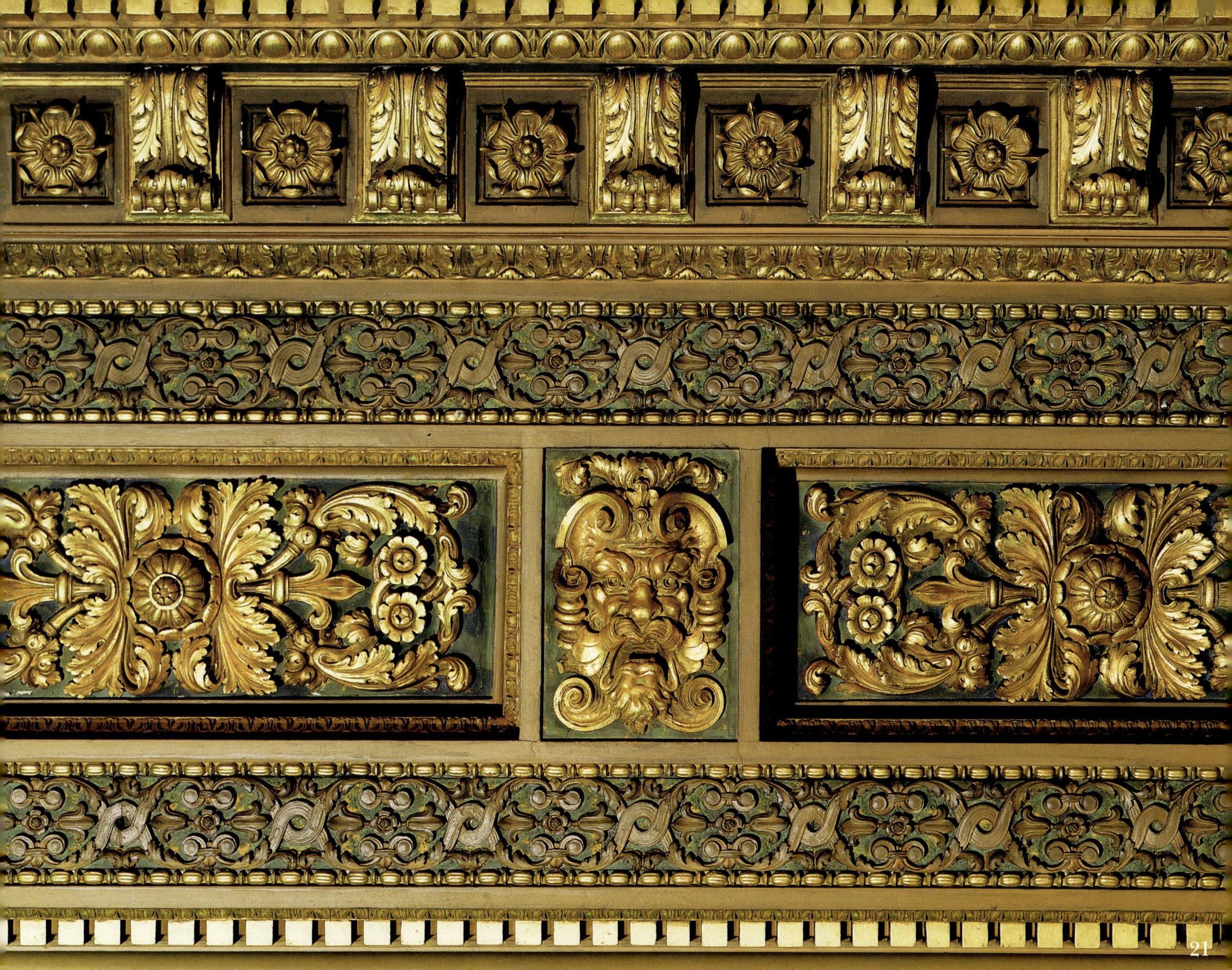

31

33

42

51

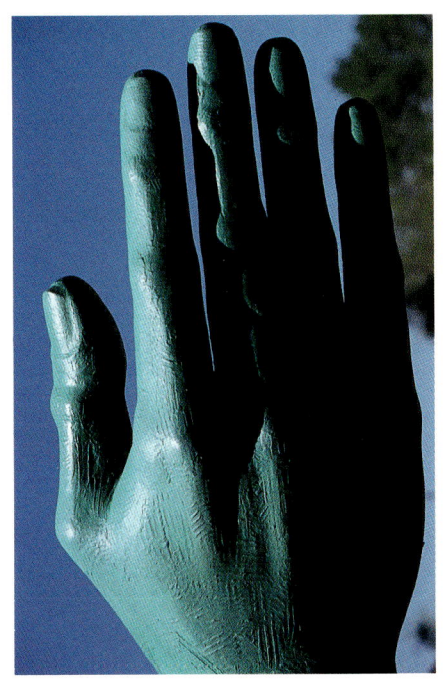

83

Page 1
CLEVELAND ON THE MOVE

―――

Page 2
WINTER SUNSET ON THE CUYAHOGA

―――

Page 3
PUBLIC SQUARE REDEFINED

―――

Page 4
GENERAL MOSES CLEAVELAND
Public Square: detail
1888
Sculptor:
James G. C. Hamilton

LIGHT UP CLEVELAND: 1989

―――

Page 5
LIGHT UP CLEVELAND: 1989

―――

Page 6
RIVERFEST 1991

CHRISTMAS IN PUBLIC SQUARE
Soldiers and Sailors Monument
1894
Sculptor: Levi Scofield

―――

Page 7
VIEW SOUTH FROM SOCIETY CENTER
Tower City Center
Public Square 1930
Architects: Graham, Anderson, Probst & White
1990 Rehabilitation: Architects: RTKL

Page 8
VIEW EAST FROM SOCIETY CENTER
BP America
1986
Architects: Hellmuth, Obata & Kassabaum

―――

Page 9
VIEW WEST FROM SOCIETY CENTER
The Flats and harbor

―――

Page 10
MAYOR'S OFFICE: TAPESTRY ROOM
Cleveland City Hall
1916
Architect: J. Milton Dyer

―――

Page 11
CITY COUNCIL CHAMBERS
Cleveland City Hall
1916
Architect: J. Milton Dyer
Mural: "Where Men and Minerals Meet"
Artist: Ivor G. Johns

―――

Page 12
ROTUNDA:
CUYAHOGA COUNTY COURT HOUSE
1912
Principal Designer: Charles Morris
Architects: Lehman & Schmitt

―――

Page 13
TURTLES:
CUYAHOGA COUNTY COURT HOUSE
Detail: Lamp standard

Page 14
JUSTICE: STAINED GLASS WINDOW
Cuyahoga County Court House

APPEALING FOR JUSTICE
Cuyahoga County Court House
Detail: Mural

―――

Page 15
ROTUNDA: CLEVELAND CITY HALL
1916
Architect: J. Milton Dyer

―――

Page 16
LOBBY: FEDERAL RESERVE BANK
1923
Architects: Walker & Weeks

―――

Page 17
FEDERAL RESERVE BANK
Detail: Rotunda, Main Lobby

―――

Page 18
WEST COURT ROOM
Federal Court House
1905-11
Architect: Arnold Brunner
Mural: "The Common Law"
Artist: H. Siddons Mobray

―――

Page 19
EAST COURT ROOM
Federal Court House
1905-11
Mural: "The Law"
Artist: Edwin Blashfield

Page 20
APPLYING GOLD LEAF
Portico, Tower City Center
Rehabilitation: 1988
Details: ceiling

―――

Page 21
EAST COURT ROOM CEILING
Federal Court House

―――

Page 22
THE AVENUE UNDER CONSTRUCTION
Tower City Center
1989

―――

Page 23
THE GRAND OPENING: THE AVENUE
Tower City Center
March 1990

―――

Page 24
THE AVENUE
Tower City Center

―――

Page 25
"TOPPING OUT" CEREMONY
Tower City Center

―――

Page 26
A NEW VIEW OF TERMINAL TOWER
Tower City Center

Page 27
FIRST CHRISTMAS: THE AVENUE
1990
Tower City Center

———

Page 28
SOCIETY CENTER
1991
Architect: Cesar Peli
van Dijk, Johnson & Partners

———

Page 29
SPACE WALK
Society Center under construction

———

Page 30
CONFERENCE
Society Center under construction

———

Page 31
TEAMWORK
Society Center under construction

WALKIN' TALL
Society Center under construction

———

Page 32
GETTIN' IT RIGHT
Society Center under construction

———

Page 33
CLIFF HANGER
Society Center under construction

STEEL MAN
Society Center under construction

Page 34
ROOM WITH A VIEW
Society Center under construction

———

Page 35
VEILED VIEW
Society Center under construction

———

Page 36
ABSTRACT I: RUBBLE CHUTE
Tower City Center under construction

———

Page 37
ABSTRACT II: NEW STEEL
Society Center under construction

———

Page 38
TOM JOHNSON
Public Square
1916
Sculptor: Herman Matzen

———

Page 39
THOMAS JEFFERSON
Cuyahoga County Court House
1913
Sculptor: Karl Bitter

———

Page 40
ROTUNDA: AMERITRUST
Tiffany window
1906
Architect: George B. Post

Page 41
AMERITRUST
1906
(Formerly Cleveland Trust)
Architect: George B. Post

———

Page 42
AWAKENING
Donald Gray Gardens
Cleveland Municipal Stadium
1936
Sculptor: William McVey

MERMAIDS
Cleveland Museum of Art
Fine Arts Garden
1929
F. Landi (Finished by Chester Beach)

———

Page 43
DONALD GRAY
GARDENS
Cleveland Municipal Stadium
1931
Design: Osborn Engineering
Architects: Walker & Weeks

———

Page 44
CLEVELAND CULTURAL GARDENS
Martin Luther King Drive
detail: Confucious:
    Chinese Cultural Garden
       1985
background: Dome
The Temple
1924
Architect: Charles R. Greco

Page 45
CLEVELAND GRAYS COLOR GUARD

CHINESE CULTURAL GARDEN
Cleveland Cultural Gardens
Martin Luther King Drive
1985
Detail: Stairs

———

Page 46
GWINN ESTATE
Home of William G. Mather
Bratenahl

———

Page 47
BELGIAN VILLAGE
1928
Village Plan: Anthony Dinardo
Architect: Harold Fullerton

———

Page 48
CHARLES F.
SCHWEINFURTH HOME
East 75th
1915
Architect: Charles F.
Schweinfurth

———

Page 49
SPRING RACING IN THE WIND
Cleveland Museum of Art
Fine Arts Garden
Sculptor: unknown

Page 50
LAKE VIEW CEMETERY

———

Page 51
UKRAINIAN CULTURAL GARDEN
Cleveland Cultural Gardens
Martin Luther King Drive
1930

ERIE STREET CEMETERY
Established 1826

———

Page 52
DINING ROOM
Hay House
1910
Western Reserve Historical Society

———

Page 53
CHAGRIN RIVER
Chagrin Falls

———

Page 54
LATE SUMMER EVENING
Walden, Aurora

———

Page 55
AUTUMN

———

Page 56
GOLDSMITH HOUSE
Hale Farm

Page 57
EASY DOES IT!
Grand Prix, Hunter, Jumper Classics
South Chagrin Metroparks
Reservation Field

———

Page 58
THREE FIGURES ON FOUR BENCHES
Justice Center
1981
Sculptor: George Segal

———

Page 59
M-K FERGUSON
(formerly United States Post Office)
1934
*Architects: Walker & Weeks and
    Philip L. Small and Associates)*
1991 Rehabilitation:
*Architects: Paul Westlake and Peter van Dijk
    of Van Dijk, Johnson & Partners*

TOWER CITY CENTER
1930
Architects: Graham, Anderson, Probst & White
1990 Rehabilitation: *RTKL*

———

Page 60
WAR MEMORIAL FOUNTAIN
1964
Sculptor: Marshall Fredericks
1991 Restoration: Society Center
Restorer: Linda Merk-Gould/Fine

SOCIETY CENTER WITH SPHERE
FROM WAR MEMORIAL FOUNTAIN

———

Page 61
WAR MEMORIAL FOUNTAIN
1964
Sculptor: Marshall Fredericks
Details: Hand/Sphere and Head

Page 62
SHAKER LAKES IN THE FALL

———

Page 63
ROW HOUSES
Prospect Avenue

———

Page 64
NINTH STREET: THE NEW LOOK
OF CLEVELAND
Ohio Bell 1984
Architects: Dalton, Dalton, Newport

One Cleveland Center
1981
Architects: Hugh Stubbins & Associates

———

Page 65
SUMMER LUNCH BREAK
Galleria
1987
Architects: Kober & Belluschi

———

Page 66
MUSIC AND COMMUNICATIONS
BUILDING
Cleveland State University
1990
Architects: van Dijk, Johnson & Partners

———

Page 67
SILHOUETTES ON PUBLIC SQUARE
One Cleveland Center
1981
Architects: Hugh Stubbins & Associates

Page 68
NORTHPOINT
1990
Architect: Jerry Payto

———

Page 69
GALLERIA
1987
Architects: Kober & Belluschi

———

Page 70
PARADE THE CIRCLE
Cleveland Museum of Art
Celebration: 75 years

———

Page 71
PARADE THE CIRCLE
Cleveland Museum of Art
Celebration: 75 years

———

Page 72
SUMMER EVENING IN THE FLATS
The Watermark Restaurant

———

Page 73
THE FLATS
Shooters

———

Page 74
RACE WEEK
Sailing on Lake Eire

Page 75
RACE WEEK
Sailing on Lake Erie

SUMMER LEISURE ON THE CUYAHOGA RIVER
Watermark Restaurant

———

Page 76
THE HEAT IS ON!

———

Page 77
ROCKY RIVER YACHT CLUB
Indian Island / Rocky River Basin

———

Page 78
THE ARCADE
1890
Firm: The Detroit Bridge Company
Architects: George H. Smith
and John Eisenmann

———

Page 79
CARNEGIE WEST LIBRARY
1910
Architect: Edward L. Tilto

Page 80
EPWORTH-EUCLID
UNITED METHODIST CHURCH
1928
Architects: Bertram Goodhue and
Walker & Weeks

ST. JOHN'S CATHEDRAL
ROMAN CATHOLIC
1852
Architect: Patrick Charles Keeley

TRINITY CATHEDRAL
1907
Architect: Charles Schweinfurth

———

Page 81
ST. THEODOSIUS RUSSIAN
ORTHODOX CATHEDRAL
1911
Architect: Frederick C. Baird

———

Page 82
BRUSH ARC LAMP
(1890)
Society Center
(formerly Society For Savings Bank)
detail: 1991 reinstallation
Architect: George B. Post

———

Page 83
BRUSH ARC LAMP
(1890)
Society Center
(formerly Society For Savings Bank)
detail: 1991 reinstallation
Architect: George B. Post

Page 84
PORTAL
1976
Sculptor: Isamu Noguchi

———

Page 85
LAST
Frank J. Lausche State
Office Building
1979
Sculptor: Tony Smith

———

Page 86
SEVERANCE HALL
1930-31
Architect: Walker & Weeks

———

Page 87
60 YEARS ON THE SQUARE!
CELEBRATION
Tower City Center
July 3, 1990

———

Page 88
SUNSET ON LAKE ERIE
West 25th Street